The SHARK
Project Book

CONTENTS

Written by Michele Hall
Photographs by Howard Hall

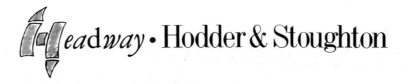
Headway · Hodder & Stoughton

My first shark

I had been a scuba diver for only a few weeks when my husband, Howard, offered to take me diving to look for sharks.

I was uneasy about the idea of coming face-to-face with an animal big and powerful enough to hurt me. After all, sharks are huge, terrifying creatures like Jaws, aren't they? But Howard assured me that we would be quite safe. He was right, and I was in for a big surprise.

We'd been swimming underwater for just a few minutes when Howard pointed towards the ocean floor. Why was he pointing down there? When I looked closely I saw an animal buried in the sand that didn't look like any shark I'd ever seen in books or on television. It was only about four feet long and it didn't have fearsome-looking teeth sticking out of its mouth. It just sat there, hiding in the sand. We swam closer, and each of us lightly stroked the top of its head. The funny-looking animal didn't attack or bite. It just lay there and ignored us.

When we got back to the beach, Howard told me that we'd seen an angel shark. He explained that there are about 350 known species of sharks, with many different characteristics. This really got me thinking. I started wondering about what makes sharks different from each other. Are sharks dangerous man-eaters or are they completely harmless, like the angel shark? Where do sharks live? What do they eat? How do they reproduce? So many questions! I decided to find out the answers. I was amazed at all that I learned.

What is a shark?

Sharks are fish. They belong to a class of fish called *Chondrichthyes*, or cartilaginous fish.

Grey reef shark

Their skeletons are made of **cartilage**, which makes them different from most other fish. Cartilage is a light, tough, elastic material, like the tissue in your ears and nose. A shark skeleton consists of a skull, a spinal column, supports for the tail and fins and a few gill arches. Sharks are held together mostly by muscle and their very tough skin. Most other fish have bony skeletons, like humans.

Rays, skates and an odd looking fish called a chimera also have skeletons made of cartilage. They too are members of the class *Chondrichthyes* and share many shark-like characteristics.

Most rays and skates have broad, flat, wing-like fins. Unlike sharks, rays and skates swim by flapping these fins, much like birds flap their wings to fly. Some rays grow to be enormous. The manta ray can grow to more than twenty feet across and may weigh nearly two tons! It soars through the ocean like a giant bird, looking for swarms of tiny plankton to eat.

If you think that dinosaurs were the first creatures on Earth, you're wrong. In fact, sharks swam in the ocean 400 million years before man appeared, and 200 million years before the first dinosaurs walked on land. However, unlike dinosaurs, sharks still exist today. Imagine an animal that has undergone 400 million years of evolution! This has resulted in an animal that is so well adapted to life in the sea that it is considered the perfect predator.

Scientists believe that two to three thousand different **species**, or kinds, of sharks once lived. Most of the earliest species died out long ago. But many ancestors of modern sharks were swimming in the ocean about 135 million years ago, and they weren't very different from the sharks living in the seas today.

Diver getting a ride on a manta ray

Different kinds of sharks

There are about 350 different species of shark roaming the seas, and another 400 species of rays and skates. Sharks are found in many different shapes and sizes.

People typically think of sharks as being big and grey, with torpedo-shaped bodies and ferocious-looking teeth. Well, not all sharks look like that. Some, like angel sharks and wobbegongs (main picture), are as flat as pancakes. This allows them to bury themselves in the sand or mud of the ocean floor, hiding so they can strike at unsuspecting prey passing above.

Other sharks have slim, stream-lined bodies which allow them to glide slowly through the water. These include thresher sharks, blue sharks, and white-tip sharks.

The stream-lined
blue shark

The hammerhead shark's name describes the shape of its head! Hammerhead sharks have uniquely flattened heads, with an eye and nostril on each end of the hammer-like protrusions. The hammerhead is perhaps the strangest-looking of all sharks.

Great white sharks, mako sharks and bull sharks are short, robust and shaped like a rugby ball. These sharks are built for strength and speed.

Great white shark

Mako shark

Bull shark

Whale sharks to pygmy sharks

Sharks are the world's largest fish. The whale shark is the biggest of all.

Another giant shark is the basking shark, which grows to more than 10 metres long. Despite their colossal size, whale sharks and basking sharks are very gentle creatures. Their teeth are very small and are not used for feeding. These enormous animals use their gills like a butterfly net, straining the water for plankton and small fish.

Not all sharks are big. The long-spined pygmy shark doesn't grow much longer than 25 centimetres, and the cookie-cutter shark is only 14 centimetres long. These, and many other small shark species, live in the deep ocean where the water is dark and cold. Some have special organs which produce a light called **bioluminescence.** They use this light to attract or locate prey and mates, or to blind and trick larger predators.

Amazing shark facts

The largest whale shark ever caught measured 12.1 metres long and weighed as much as a bus!

eft: Basking shark
ight: Whale shark

How do sharks get around?

You can tell how fast a shark can swim by looking at the shape of its fins and tail.

Many sharks, like the blue shark, are gliders. They have sleek narrow bodies, long graceful **pectoral**, or chest, fins and **heterocercal** tails. A heterocercal tail means that the top lobe of the tail is larger than the bottom lobe. The top lobe helps push the shark's tail down, which then helps keep the shark's nose up. This allows the slower swimmers to plane through the water in a slightly nose-up position, so they won't sink. The long pectoral fins act like wings, allowing a slow-swimming shark to plane through the water with minimal effort.

The fastest, most powerful sharks, like the mako and great white, are built like jet fighters. They have thick, muscular bodies and forceful, crescent-shaped tails. Because they move so fast, they don't need extra help in keeping a nose-up position, so they have **homocercal** tails – the top and bottom lobes are of nearly equal size. Like jet fighter planes, the thick, torpedo-shaped bodies of great whites and makos have short, stubby pectoral fins that produce very little drag at high speed.

Many sharks spend most of their time hiding in the reef or buried in sand, instead of swimming around. Angel sharks, horn sharks and swell sharks are 'bottom dwellers'. They don't move very fast or very far at one time. Their soft, round fins are better adapted to their slower life-style. When they swim, their bodies sway back and forth from their nose to their tail as they slowly move along in an almost snake-like fashion.

Sink or swim?

If sharks aren't swimming, they're either resting on the ocean floor or sinking. Their bodies are heavier than water, even though their cartilaginous skeletons are lighter than the bony skeletons of other fish. But bony fish have an organ called a **swimbladder** which they can inflate with gas to keep them afloat. With a swimbladder, a fish is able to stay suspended at any level in the water. It's like having an internal balloon! But since sharks don't have swimbladders, they must either swim or sink to the bottom of the sea.

Sharks get some help from their large, oil-filled livers. Oil floats in water, so their oily livers give them additional buoyancy. But even sharks with large oil-filled livers are heavier than water and will sink if they stop swimming.

The epaulette shark is a bottom dweller

Do sharks ever stop swimming?

It's commonly thought that all sharks must swim continuously in order to keep life-giving oxygen flowing through their gills. But if this were true, what would the bottom dwellers like the angel sharks, swell sharks and horn sharks do?

Amazing shark facts

The furthest recorded shark migration is by a blue shark: a journey of 5,980 km from New York state to Brazil.

Caribbean reef shark

It's true that all sharks need to have a continually replenished supply of water running through their gills. As sharks swim about, oxygen-rich water flows in through their mouths, over their gills and out through their gill slits. Oxygen is absorbed into their blood stream as water runs over the gills. Bottom-dwelling species don't need to swim to keep water moving over their gills, however. They have special muscles which continuously pump water in through their mouths and out through their gill slits. But many of the larger open ocean sharks, such as the blue, mako, and great white, don't have these muscles and must constantly swim to stay alive. They swim from the moment of their birth until they die, which may be more than sixty years.

How fast do sharks swim?

Although they're efficient swimmers, most sharks are slow when compared to speedier fish like tuna. Most *pelagic*, or open-ocean, sharks generally cruise at less than 5 km per hour. However, some, like the mako shark, can accelerate to 48 km per hour for short periods. Those that are capable of these high speeds can seldom maintain such velocities for more than a minute or so. When a shark starts swimming fast, it uses energy stored in its muscles. This energy quickly runs out and the shark must slow down while more energy is absorbed into its bloodstream.

The author with an angel shark

What about those teeth?

Shark teeth are very different from human teeth.

Unlike human teeth, shark teeth are not attached directly to the jaw. Instead, they grow from a special membrane of the skin called the *tooth bed.* Shark teeth are worn away constantly and are replaced by new ones. Behind the front row, sharks have 5 to 15 rows of back-up teeth. When a shark tooth falls out or breaks off, another moves forward to fill in the gap, sometimes within 24 hours.

Not all species of sharks eat the same things or catch food in the same way. Therefore, their teeth vary greatly in shape from species to species. For example, mako sharks strike at their fast-moving prey quickly, using their teeth to inflict as much damage as possible. Their teeth work well to snare fast-swimming fish, but are not very suitable for

tearing chunks out of large prey, so they normally swallow their prey whole. In contrast, horn sharks live on the bottom of the ocean and feed on crabs, molluscs and sea urchins. Some of their teeth are modified into hard plates for crushing these hard-shelled animals.

The teeth of great white sharks, on the

other hand, are robust and triangular with serrated edges. They work fearsomely well for tearing big chunks out of large prey.

In fact, a shark's entire body is covered by tiny teeth called dermal denticles, which makes their skin very rough. It might seem that very smooth skin would be best for gliding through water. But rough shark skin actually reduces water turbulence and drag, allowing sharks to swim with less effort.

How does a shark bite?

Depending on the species, a shark's mouth is in one of two places. A **terminal** mouth is at the front of the shark's head, and its snout doesn't protrude in front of it. Whale sharks, angel sharks, and wobbegongs have this kind of mouth.

Most sharks have a **subterminal** mouth,

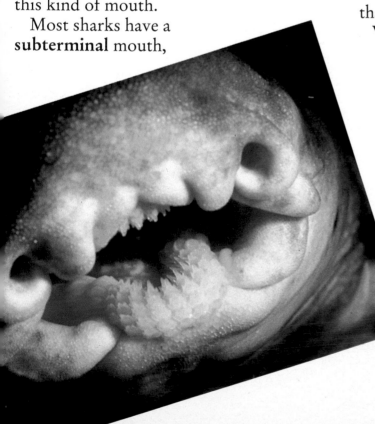

which is located on the **ventral**, or underside, of the head. These sharks have snouts that protrude out in front of their mouths. White-tip sharks, blue sharks and hammerheads have subterminal mouths. You might think that a long snout, protruding far in front of its mouth would get in the way when a shark attacks. This is not so. When a shark attacks, it dislocates its jaw from its skull. This allows its jaw and all those teeth to lunge forward out past the end of its nose. Once the prey is grasped, it is pulled into the mouth and the jaw returns to its original position. And all this happens in the blink of an eye!

How do sharks find prey?

Sharks combine many sensory systems to explore their environment, go after their prey and avoid being eaten themselves.

Humans have five senses – hearing, taste, sight, touch, and smell. Sharks use the same senses we use, but they also have a few more.

Smell

Sharks use their keen sense of smell to detect many different scents in the water. One of these is blood. Studies show that sharks can detect very small amounts of blood in the ocean, sometimes as little as one part per one hundred million. This is the same as one drop of blood mixed in over a thousand gallons of sea water!

Sight

Sharks' eyes are much more sensitive to light than ours are. A structure in the eye called the **tapetum lucidum** reflects incoming light back through the eye. This allows sharks to see in near darkness which helps them feed at night or in the deep ocean.

Instead of an eyelid like ours, many sharks have a **nictitating membrane.** This movable eyelid-like flap of skin protects the eye from damage when the shark is feeding. In the last moment before the shark attacks, the membrane covers the eye, which shields it from being punctured by the struggling prey.

Hearing

Sharks both 'hear' and 'feel' sound. They use internal ears to 'hear' the low frequency vibrations made by wounded and struggling fish. They can also 'feel' sound waves and vibrations with a sensory system called the **lateral line.**

The lateral line is composed of a series of nerve receptors located beneath the skin. These receptors form a line running along the sides of the shark's body, upper tail and around its head. Using its lateral line, a shark can 'feel' vibrations produced by an injured and struggling fish over a mile away!

Ampullae of Lorenzini

Most sharks have sensory organs covering many parts of their heads and snouts called **ampullae of Lorenzini.** These special organs allow sharks to detect very weak electrical fields in water.

Why do sharks need to detect electrical fields? It helps them catch their prey. The muscles and circulatory systems of fish and other animals create weak electrical fields. When a shark is within a few feet of its prey, it can detect this electrical field. In this way the shark can hunt prey in absolute darkness and very murky water, or when prey is hiding beneath sand.

What do sharks eat?

There are all sorts of stories about sharks eating everything from tin cans to licence plates.

Well, people have been known to eat strange things, too!

Sharks normally eat other sea life. Each shark species is designed for hunting specific kinds of prey. For instance, mako sharks tend to eat fast-swimming tuna and mackerel, while blue sharks eat slower-swimming fish and squid. Bottom-dwellers like horn sharks go after crabs and urchins, and white sharks prefer to dine on sea lions and seals.

The two largest species of sharks survive on an almost microscopic diet. Whale sharks and basking sharks suck tons of water into their mouths and filter out tiny plankton for their nourishment.

How often a shark eats depends on its level of activity, its *metabolic rate* (how efficiently the shark utilizes the food it eats) and how deep it lives in the ocean. Some sharks, like shortfin makos, are active hunters and may catch a meal every day, eating several times their body weight each year. White sharks, on the other hand, may patrol vast areas of the sea eating a single meal, such as a sea lion, every few weeks. But then, eating a 400 pound sea lion is a pretty big meal! Sharks that live in the deep ocean, where the water is near freezing, have very slow metabolic rates and may sometimes go a month or more between meals.

Amazing shark facts

The average life span of a shark is about 25 years. But some may live between 70 and 100 years.

Shark reproduction and baby sharks

The way shark eggs are fertilized is different than the way most other fish eggs are fertilized.

Most female bony fish lay thousands of eggs in nests or release clouds of eggs into the water. The eggs are then fertilized by the male. Thousands of very tiny **larvae** (tiny undeveloped baby fish), are later born. Because they are so small and fragile, only a small percentage of them survive.

Shark eggs are fertilized *inside* the female shark. When baby sharks, or **pups**, are born, they are thousands of times larger than fish larvae and are very well developed. Their large size increases their chance for survival.

While shark **embryos**, or unborn baby sharks, are developing, they need lots of nourishment. There are three different ways that shark embryos are nourished before they are born – **oviparity**, **ovoviviparity** and **viviparity**.

Oviparity is the most primitive way that shark embryos develop. The female shark lays a few very large fertilized eggs on the sea floor. These eggs are protected by very tough, leathery casings. It takes an exceptionally long time for these eggs to hatch. Some lie on the ocean floor for more than a year before hatching! During that time, the shark embryo receives its nourishment from a large yolk which is also inside the casing.

Most shark eggs are laid by small bottom-dwelling species, like the horn shark and swell shark. But the largest shark in the world – the whale shark – also lays eggs. The egg of the whale shark measures over fifty centimetres (one foot) in length, and when the baby whale shark hatches it is over 14 inches long! Whale shark eggs are very rare. Only one has ever been found. It was caught in a fishing net in the Gulf of Mexico in 1953.

A swell shark hatches

Ovoviviparity is the most common type of reproduction in sharks. The female shark creates an egg, but she doesn't lay it. Instead, she retains it inside her body until the egg hatches. Just like oviparous sharks, the embryos get their nourishment from the yolks. But when the yolk is gone, the baby sharks get hungry. The strongest of the baby sharks then begin eating their smaller and weaker brothers and sisters! This behaviour is *not* recommended for human children! Usually only one shark pup is still alive by the time the mother is ready to give birth. Ovoviviparous sharks include some bottom-dwellers like angle sharks, and pelagics like basking sharks and sand tigers.

Viviparity is the most advanced type of shark reproduction. It is also the one most like mammal reproduction. The embryos develop inside the mother's uterus for many months. Each embryo has a yolk and an umbilical cord which attaches to a placenta. Much like human embryos, the growing shark embryos get nutrients from the mother through an umbilical cord. Lemon and blue are among the species of sharks born this way.

Lemon shark

Sand tiger shark

Man-eaters versus shark-eaters

There's a common belief that sharks are man-eaters, and that if you see one in the ocean you're doomed to be eaten alive.

This myth was made more believable in the 1970s by Peter Benchley's book and the subsequent film *Jaws.*

I remember when *Jaws* first came out. I was afraid to go scuba diving and the last thing I wanted to do was see a shark. I later learned that more people die from honey bee stings than are killed by sharks! Of course, it's wise to be careful around sharks.

The most dangerous are probably white sharks, tiger sharks and bull sharks. But even attacks by these sharks are very rare. On average, there are only one hundred shark attacks worldwide per year.

Most shark attacks are cases of mistaken identity. A diver or a swimmer is mistaken for something the shark usually eats. Often the water is murky, and the shark bites thinking it has found a fish or a sea lion. When the shark tastes a human instead, it almost always spits it out and swims away. Most attacks are not fatal – 65-75 per cent of people attacked by sharks survive.

Shark attacks can be provoked by something the swimmer or diver is doing. Sometimes the shark is defending its territory when a diver tries to get too close for a good look or to take a photograph.

Sharks can also be attracted to the sounds and smells produced by spearfishing. As the shark comes in for dinner, the diver may just be in the way!

Amazing shark facts

Sixty-two per cent of shark attacks occur in less than five feet of water.

Shark protection

A variety of mechanical defences against sharks have been tried over the years. Some underwater photographers wear a steel mesh suit when diving with sharks. Usually, the photographers have used bait to attract the sharks, and the presence of fish blood in the water increases the chances of attack. The steel mesh suit simply prevents the shark's teeth from penetrating to the skin. It works well with relatively small sharks like the blue, but doesn't offer much protection against really large sharks like the great white.

Southern Australia is home to a large population of great white sharks. It's also a great place to find a valuable and tasty mollusc called the abalone. Abalone are gathered by divers. Some abalone divers move about in small cages while collecting abalone. The cages protect the divers from attack by great whites.

Forms of naturally-occurring protection have also been studied. Dr Eugenie Clark from the United States discovered a fish in the Red Sea called the Moses sole. This fish is capable of secreting a milky fluid that sharks find distasteful. Other marine animals may also produce natural shark repellents. Some sea cucumbers have a protective secretion that affects sharks' smell and taste receptors. Scientists find these naturally-occurring shark repellents interesting, but they doubt that any of these chemicals will be used to produce shark repellents for humans. The truth is that shark attacks are so rare, there is little need for shark repellents.

Amazing shark facts
The steel mesh suit worn by some professional divers is made up of over 400,000 tiny, interlocking steel rings.

Shark-eating humans

Humans are far more dangerous to sharks than sharks are to humans.

Humans kill about 100 million sharks each year. Many, about half, are eaten. Others are killed in gill-nets, which are designed to catch other fish. These sharks are thrown back into the ocean as waste. Some sharks are caught just for their fins, which are removed to make shark-fin soup, and the rest of the shark is tossed back into the sea to die. Worst of all, many sharks are killed just for fun.

Sharks grow and reproduce slowly, so they can't survive unregulated and indiscriminate fishing. Sadly, overfishing is causing

shark populations to decline in most oceans of the world.

Should we care if there are no more sharks? I think we should! Sharks are important predators that help keep life in the ocean in balance. These wonderful creatures are part of our wilderness. They help make life on Earth more fascinating.

Certainly sharks can be dangerous. But so can lions, tigers and elephants. Yet people all over the world are sorry to see these animals disappear from the African plain. And someday soon, if overfishing continues, causing sharks to vanish from our seas, I think people will be sorry to see them go as well.

Index

British Library Cataloguing in Publication Data

A catalogue record for this book is available from the British Library.

ISBN 0 340 57621 9

First published 1993
Impression number   10 9 8 7 6 5 4 3
Year   1998 1997 1996 1995 1994 1993

Typeset by Litho Link Ltd, Welshpool, Powys, Wales.
Printed in Hong Kong for the educational publishing division of Hodder & Stoughton Ltd, Mill Road, Dunton Green, Sevenoaks, Kent by Colorcraft.

Acknowledgements

The author and publishers would like to thank Ardea London Ltd for their permission to reproduce the photographs of the Bull Shark on page 9 and on the front cover.

All other photographs courtesy of Howard Hall